SCHOLASTIC

50 Fill-In Math Word Problems

TIME & MEASUREMENT

Grades 2–3

by Bob Krech and Joan Novelli

New York • Toronto • London • Auckland • Sydney
Mexico City • New Delhi • Hong Kong • Buenos Aires

Teaching *Resources*

Thanks to Andrew and Faith for laughing

Editor: Joan Novelli
Cover design by Jason Robinson
Interior design by Holly Grundon
Interior illustrations by Teresa Anderko

ISBN-13: 978-0-545-07483-4
ISBN-10: 0-545-07483-5

Contents

Fill-In Math Word Problems

About This Book

When we learn to read, we learn to recognize the letters of the alphabet, we practice letter-sound relationships, and we learn punctuation, but what it's all about is eventually being able to read text. A similar situation exists in math. We learn to recognize and write numerals, what the symbols mean, and we learn operations such as addition and subtraction, but what it's all about is what you can do with these skills—applying what you know to solve problems. *50 Fill-In Math Word Problems: Time & Measurement* provides lots of funny stories—and some very interesting problems to solve.

What Are Fill-In Math Word Problems?

A fill-in math word problem is a funny story with a math problem waiting to happen. Most of the word problem is already supplied, but a few key words have been removed and replaced with blanks, just like in some other word games. Students fill in those blanks with missing nouns, adjectives, verbs, and other types of words. The difference is that this game is missing some numbers as well. When students supply the missing numbers along with the words, they suddenly have a wacky, math word problem that's fun to read and solve!

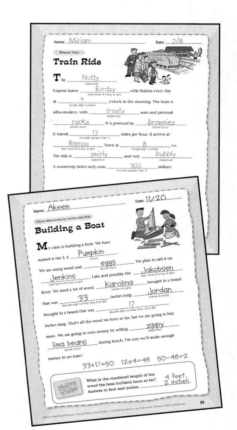

Why Use Fill-In Math Word Problems?

Traditional math word problems can provide a meaningful context for students to apply their skills, but sometimes the problems can be a bit boring. Remember trying to figure out when the two trains would pass each other? That won't happen with *50 Fill-In Math Word Problems*. Students help create these wacky word problems, which provide for plenty of good problem-solving practice with grade-appropriate skills and concepts related to the content areas of time and measurement. Have fun while doing math? Absolutely!

Teaching With Fill-In Math Word Problems

You can choose a fill-in story to use with the entire class, or select as many as needed to match different ability levels of students. For instance, you might have some students who would benefit from practice with time to the hour, while others may be ready for the challenge of calculating elapsed time. (For connections to the math standards, see Meeting the Math Standards, page 12.) Whatever the need, there is a set of fill-in stories to support it. The stories in this book are organized by skills as follows:

- Time to the Hour
- Time to the Half Hour
- Time to the Quarter Hour
- Time to the Minute
- Elapsed Time
- Linear Measurement: Inches and Feet

- Linear Measurement: Feet and Yards
- Linear Measurement: Centimeters and Meters
- Linear Measurement: Perimeter and Area
- Weight Measurement: Ounces and Pounds
- Weight Measurement: Grams and Kilograms
- Liquid Measurement: Ounces–Gallons
- Liquid Measurement: Milliliters and Liters

Teaching Tips

When teaching with the stories in this book, be sure to review and reinforce the following strategies with students.

- Time is very much at home in a study of measurement. Help students understand that with time measurements, they can't just add the numbers together and get a sensible answer. For example, with "Cleaning Up" (page 28), if we say John started his chores at 2:30 and it took him 15 minutes to clean one room and 30 minutes to clean the other, to figure out when he finished we can't simply add those numbers (2:30 + 15 + 30), or we would get 2:75. There is no such time! Remind students that, with measurements of time, once they have sixty minutes, they need to convert to an hour, very similar to regrouping tens and ones when adding.

- The measurement problems in this book emphasize an understanding of both standard and metric measurement units, such as inches, feet, centimeters, meters, cups, quarts, and liters. It's probably not necessary to have measuring tools such as scales and rulers for everyone, but you may want to have one or two appropriate tools to use for demonstrations and to enable students to prove that their answers are correct. It's also helpful when students are working on these problems to supply them with individual measurement reference charts showing names of units of measure, abbreviations, and equivalencies. Or, display a poster containing this information for reference.

Modeling the Process

Before expecting students to do the stories on their own, model how to complete a story and solve the problem. Use an overhead to project the story so students can follow along. Invite a student to help you out, and follow these steps:

1. Starting at the beginning of the story, read the prompts for the fill-ins—for instance, "adjective." Write in the adjective your helper suggests—for example, *stinky*.

2. When you have filled in all of the blanks, read aloud the story, beginning with the title.

3. Read aloud "Solve This!" and think aloud as you use information from the story to solve the problem. (This is a good time to model how to use the Fantastic Five-Step Process in your think aloud. See page 9 for more information.)

How to Fill in the Blanks

Each fill-in math word problem requires students to fill in a set of words or numbers to complete the story. They will then use some of the information they provide to solve the problem. Following is more detailed information about how to fill in the blanks.

Choosing Words

From singular and plural nouns to verbs and adjectives, different kinds of words are required to fill in the blanks of the stories. Review each type of word with students, using the Word Choice Chart (page 13) as a guide. To help students create their own handy references, have them complete the third column of their chart with additional examples of each type of fill-in. They can refer to this when completing stories as a reminder of what kinds of words they can use. You might also consider transferring the descriptions and examples to a wall chart for easy reference.

Note that, at times, students will also have to fill in other types of words, such as the name of a girl, boy, or famous person, a type of animal, or a color. These are not included in the chart as they are already specific enough to support students in their word choice. When you introduce any new story to students, just take a moment to review all of the types of words they may need to use.

Choosing Numbers

Each fill-in math word problem specifies different types of numbers—for example, "Going to the Game" (page 15) asks for a "single-digit number greater than 0" and a "number greater than 1", while "Doghouse" (page 44) specifies a "double-digit number" for two of the blanks. Other stories, such as "Cooking Tips" (page 20) specify a range ("number from 1 to 12"). In this case, students may choose any of the following numbers: 1, 2, 3, 4, 5, 6, 7, 8, 9, 10, 11, or 12.

You may choose to let students fill in numbers according to the directions in the stories, or you can vary the parameters to provide for differentiation of instruction, individualizing the problems for students by using the number ranges that make sense for them. For example, if a story specifies a double-digit number, you might simplify the math by changing this to read "a double-digit number from 10 to 20." If you do change the fill-in prompts in this way, be sure to check for other numbers in the story that may also need to be changed. However, keep in mind that leaving the number size open-ended to some extent is an interesting option and will provide information as to students' ability to work with different-size numbers.

Lesson Formats

There are many ways to use the stories in *50 Fill-In Math Word Problems* in your classroom. Here are a few suggestions for lesson formats.

1. Problem-Solving Partners

Have students pair up. Make copies of a fill-in story and distribute to one student in each pair. These students are the Readers. Without revealing the title (or any parts) of the story, Readers ask their partners for the missing words in order ("name of a town," "single-digit number greater than 1," "adjective," and so on) and fill in the appropriate blanks with their partners' responses. When all of the blanks are filled in, the Reader reads the completed story. The resulting silly story now contains a math word problem! Partners solve the problem (together or independently), sharing strategies and checking their answers.

2. Class Stories

Choose a story and let students take turns supplying words or numbers to fill in the blanks (again, just read the fill-in prompts in order, but do not reveal the story at this point). Fill in the blanks, and when the story is complete, read it to the class. Have students take notes on the numbers in the story and the problem they need to solve. (Or write this information on chart paper for them.) Students can work together as a class, with a partner, or independently to solve the problem. As a follow-up, let students share answers and discuss solution strategies.

3. Story Switcheroo

After students fill in the blanks for a story with a partner, make copies and distribute to the class for extra practice or homework. Twenty different versions of one story mean 20 different problems to solve! And students will love seeing their work used as a teaching tool!

4. Math Practice Pages

Invite pairs of students to create stories for a binder full of practice pages. They fill in the stories as described in "Problem-Solving Partners" (page 7), but write the answer and an explanation on the back of the paper. For extra practice, students can take a story from the binder, solve the problem, and check their answer on the back. They can then return the story to the binder.

5. Create New Stories

Creating new fill-in math word problems is another option for practicing math skills—and a motivating way to connect writing and math. Using the stories in this book as models, invite students to write their own wacky, fill-in math word problems. With students' permission, copy the stories and distribute to the class for homework (or in-class practice). Guide students in following these steps to create their stories.

- Identify a skill area and write this at the top of the paper. (You may choose to specify a skill area for students to target, such as "Time to the Half Hour," or leave this up to students to decide.)

- Brainstorm story ideas. Everyday events, such as lunchtime or recess, can make for very funny stories. Think about how measurement might fit into the story. For example, in a story about an extra long recess, the math problem might be to find out what time the kids finally had to go in. For a story about a new playground, the math problem might require finding out the area of the space.

- Write a draft of your story. Do not try to make your story "funny." Just write about an everyday event, such as toothbrushing, as if you were telling someone else about it. When you're finished, underline some of the numbers, verbs, adjectives, and nouns. After underlining them, erase the original number or word and substitute a fill-in line. Label the type of number or word beneath each fill-in line. Be sure to set up a math problem in the story.

- Write the problem to be solved at the bottom of the page. Label it "Solve This!" Solve the problem yourself to make sure it works.

- Draw a picture to illustrate the story.

Teaching Problem-Solving Skills:

The Fantastic Five-Step Process

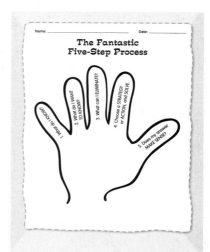

Problem solving is the first process standard listed in the National Council of Teachers Mathematics (NCTM) *Principles and Standards for Mathematics.* The accompanying statement reads, "Problem solving is an integral part of all mathematics learning. In everyday life and in the workplace, being able to solve problems can lead to great advantages. However, solving problems is not only a goal of learning mathematics but also a major means of doing so. Problem solving should not be an isolated part of the curriculum but should involve all Content Standards." In other words, in mathematics, problem solving is what it's all about!

What do you do when you first encounter a math word problem? This is what we need to help students deal with. We need to help them develop a process that they can use effectively to solve any type of math word problem. Word problems often intimidate students because there may be a lot of information, the information is embedded in text, and unlike a regular equation, it is not always clear exactly what you are supposed to do. When using these fill-in math word problems, you may want to take some time to teach (and subsequently review) the Fantastic Five-Step Process for problem solving.

The Fantastic Five-Step Process helps students approach problem solving in a logical, systematic way. No matter what type of problem students encounter, these five steps will help them through it. Learning and using the five steps will help students organize their interpretation and thinking about the problem. This is the key to good problem solving—organizing for action. The best way to help students understand the process is to demonstrate it as you work through a problem on the whiteboard or overhead. Make a copy of the graphic organizer on page 14. You can enlarge this to poster size or provide students with individual copies to follow along as you take them through an introductory lesson.

Step 1: What Do I Know?

Begin by writing a problem on the board or overhead. For example:

> Good news! Our class will have an extra long recess today!
> Lunch is at the regular time, 12 P.M. And we'll go out for recess
> at the regular time, too, which is 12:30 P.M. But instead of
> coming in at 1:00 P.M., we can stay out today for an extra 30
> minutes! What time is recess over today?

Read the problem carefully. What are the facts? Have students volunteer these orally. Write them on the board:

> Lunch is at 12 P.M.
>
> Recess starts at 12:30 P.M.
>
> Recess is usually over at 1 P.M.
>
> Recess is an extra 30 minutes today.

Encourage students to write down the facts, too. This will help them focus on what's important while looking for ways to put it in a more accessible form.

Step 2: What Do I Want to Know?

What is the question in the problem? What are we trying to find out? It's a good idea to have students state the question and also determine how the answer will be labeled. For example:

> For this problem, we want to know what time recess
> is over today.
>
> The answer will be stated as a measure of time, in hours
> and minutes, and labeled A.M. or P.M.

Step 3: What Can I Eliminate?

Once we know what we are trying to find out, we can decide what is unimportant. We may need all the information, but often enough there is extra information that can be put aside to help focus on the facts—for example:

> We can eliminate the fact that lunch is at 12:00 P.M. We don't
> need that information to answer the question.

Step 4: Choose a Strategy or Action and Solve.

Is there an action in the story (for example, is something being "taken away" or is something being "added") that will help the problem-solver decide on an operation or a way to solve the problem?

> If recess is usually over at 1:00 P.M., but today we get an extra 30 minutes, we can solve the problem by adding 30 minutes on to 1:00, so the answer is 1:30 P.M.

Step 5: Does My Answer Make Sense?

Re-read the problem. Look at the answer. Is it reasonable? Is it a sensible answer given what we know?

> It makes sense for a number of reasons. The regular recess starts at 12:30 P.M. and ends at 1:00 P.M. If we get an extra 30 minutes of recess today, that's the same as half an hour. Half past 1:00 P.M. is 1:30 P.M.—the answer we got. Another way to look at this is that recess usually lasts for 30 minutes and today we get an extra 30 minutes. That means recess is 60 minutes, or one hour! We know recess starts at 12:30 P.M., so we can figure out what 60 minutes or one hour from then is: 1:30 P.M. So, yes, our answer makes sense.

Try a couple of sample word problems using this "talk through" format with students. You might invite students to try the problem themselves first and then review step-by-step together, sharing solutions to see if all steps were considered and if solutions are, in fact, correct. Practicing the process in this way helps make it part of a student's way of thinking mathematically.

Note that there are no answer keys for the fill-in math word problems as answers will vary depending on the numbers students supply to fill in the blanks. You might set up a buddy system for checking answers or have students turn in their stories for you to check. The fill-in stories provide good opportunities to reinforce estimating strategies as they apply to determining if an answer is reasonable.

Meeting the Math Standards

The activities in this book include math content designed to support you in meeting the following math standards for measurement across grades 2–3, as outlined by the National Council of Teachers of Mathematics (NCTM) in *Principles and Standards for School Mathematics.*

Measurement

Understand measurable attributes of objects and the units, systems, and processes of measurement and apply appropriate techniques to determine measurements

- recognize attributes of length, volume, weight, area, and time and compare and order objects according to these attributes

- understand how to measure using nonstandard and standard units

- use repetition of a single unit to measure something larger than the unit

- make comparisons and estimates

The word problems in this book also support the NCTM process standards as follows.

Problem Solving

- solve problems that arise in mathematics and other contexts
- apply and adapt a variety of appropriate strategies to solve problems

Reasoning and Proof

- select and use various types of reasoning and methods of proof

Communication

- communicate mathematical thinking coherently and clearly

Connections

- understand how mathematical ideas interconnect and build on one another
- recognize and apply mathematics in contexts outside of mathematics

Representation

- create and use representations to organize, record, and communicate mathematical ideas
- use representations to model and interpret physical, social, and mathematical phenomena

Source: *Principles and Standards for School Mathematics* (National Council of Teachers of Mathematics, 2000-2004); www.standards.nctm.org.

Vocabulary-Building Connections

Take advantage of vocabulary-building opportunities that these fill-in stories present. For example, in the story "Amazing Rescue" (page 31), students will encounter the word *canyon*. To guide students in recognizing this word, you might encourage them to continue beyond the first mention of the word (in the first sentence of the story) to look for meaning clues. For example, in the second sentence students will encounter a helpful context clue ("at the bottom of the canyon"). Together with the illustration that supports the text, students will then likely recognize the word and its meaning.

Word Choice Chart

Type of Word	What It Is	More Examples
Adjective	A word that describes something, such as *smelly, happy, fierce, hilarious,* and *huge.*	
Adverb	A word that tells how something is done, such as *quickly, sadly, sleepily,* and *carefully.*	
Exclamation	A word that expresses something like *surprise, anger,* or *pain.* Examples are *Ouch! Yikes! Wow!* and *Oh!*	
Noun	A word that names a person, place, or thing, such as *teacher, telescope,* and *sandwich.*	
Plural Noun	A word that names more than one, such as *teachers, telescopes,* and *sandwiches.*	
Present-Tense Verb	A word that names an action like *run, catch, eat,* and *hop.*	
Verb Ending in *-ing*	A word that tells what is happening, like *running, catching, eating,* and *hopping.*	
Past-Tense Verb	A word that tells what has already happened, like *ran, caught, ate,* and *hopped.*	

The Fantastic Five-Step Process

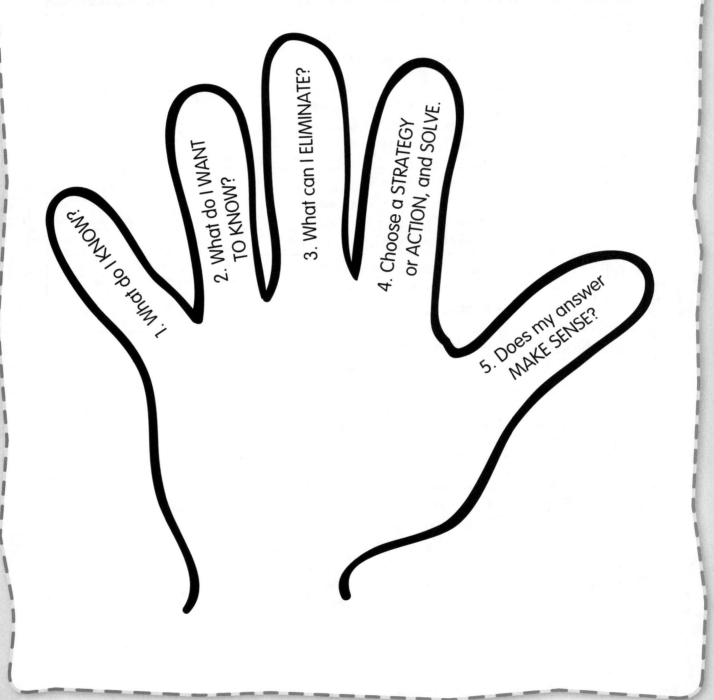

1. What do I KNOW?

2. What do I WANT TO KNOW?

3. What can I ELIMINATE?

4. Choose a STRATEGY or ACTION, and SOLVE.

5. Does my answer MAKE SENSE?

Name: _____ Date: _____

Going to the Game

My older brother, _____,
(first name of a boy)

took me to see a basketball game on

_____ night. Our favorite team, the New York
(day of the week)

_____, was playing. We wore our _____
(plural noun)   (color)

and _____ _____ to show we are
(color)   (type of clothing, plural)

big fans. I even wore a big _____ on my head! The
(noun)

game started right on time. I could see from the clock that the hour

hand was on the _____ and the minute hand
(single-digit number greater than 0)

was on the 12. Two hours later, the game was over. Our favorite player,

_____, scored _____ points.
(first and last name of a boy or girl)   (number greater than 1)

What a perfectly _____ night!
(adjective)

Solve This! What time did the game end? _____

Name: _____   Date: _____

Time to the Hour

Journey to Space

Commander _____
(last name of a famous person)

and a crew are off to Planet

_____ in the Space
(last name of a boy or girl)

Shuttle _____. Their destination is _____
(noun)   (number greater than 1)

miles away. When they left, their chronographs showed the hour hand on

_____ and the minute hand on the 12. They traveled
(single-digit number greater than 0)

for _____ hours and then took a one-hour break at
(number from 2 to 5)

_____, where they enjoyed the _____.
(name of a restaurant)   (type of food)

In one hour, they will arrive at their destination. Then they can explore the giant

_____ and beautiful _____.
(plural noun)   (plural noun)

What time will the space shuttle
arrive at its destination? _____

 50 Fill-In Math Word Problems: Time & Measurement: Grades 2–3 © 2009 by Bob Krech and Joan Novelli, Scholastic Teaching Resources

Name: _____   Date: _____

Cake Baking

I baked a cake for

_____'s
(name of a boy)

_____ birthday. I know he
(ordinal number)

likes _____ icing and _____ filling,
(flavor)   (type of fruit)

so that's the kind I made. I also put in some _____and
(plural noun)

sprinkled some _____ on top as a special treat. That should
(plural noun)

make it taste really _____. I put the cake in the oven at
(adjective)

_____ A.M. and baked it for _____
(number 1 to 12)   (choose a number: 2, 3, or 4)

hours. When he saw it, he was so surprised he _____!
(verb ending in -ed)

What time was
the cake done? _____

Name: _____ Date: _____

My New Job

I got a summer job so I can earn money

to buy a new _____.
(noun)

I am working for Mrs. _____
(last name of a famous person)

and get paid _____ an hour. I start every day at
(money amount)

_____ A.M. I finish at _____ P.M.
(single-digit number greater than 1)   (single-digit number greater than 1)

First I clean the _____ around her house. I also
(plural noun)

cut the _____. Last week I also took care of her
(plural noun)

_____ while she went shopping. That wasn't too
(noun)

_____. My favorite part of the job is organizing her
(adjective)

_____. That is so _____, I could do
(plural noun)   (adjective)

it for hours.

Solve This! How many hours
a day is the job? _____

50 Fill-In Math Word Problems: Time & Measurement: Grades 2–3 © 2009 by Bob Krech and Joan Novelli, Scholastic Teaching Resources

Name: _____   Date: _____

Amazing Stunt

My cousin _____
                                    (name of a boy)

is really _____.
                          (adjective)

He is only _____ years old,
              (number greater than 1)

but he has already started his own

_____ team.
              (type of activity)

He was also on the *Amazing Stunts* TV show. He balanced a large

_____ on his _____! He started at
            (noun)   (name of a body part)

_____ o'clock in the morning and did it for 30 minutes.
  (single-digit number greater than 1)

He set a new world record and won _____ dollars!
                                          (number greater than 1)

**What time did
the stunt end?** _____

Name: _____   Date: _____

Cooking Tips

_____
(first and last name of a girl)

is sharing cooking tips today at

_____'s Supermarket.
(last name of a famous person)

She is showing how to cook _____. I always thought
(type of food, plural)

it was too hard because they are so _____
(adjective)

and _____. But she said "It's quick and
(adjective)

_____. Just watch!" First, she put them in a big
(adjective)

_____. The she added a pinch of _____.
(type of container)   (type of seasoning)

At _____ o'clock she put it on the stove to cook for
(number from 1 to 12)

90 minutes. When it was finished it was _____
(color)

and _____. I could tell it was going to taste
(adjective)

_____!
(adjective)

Solve This!   What time was
the dish done? _____

Name: _____   Date: _____

Take the Bus

The best way to get from

_____ to
(name of a place)

_____ is to
(name of a place)

take the bus. On the bus you can sit back and

_____. You can read the _____
(present-tense verb)   (noun)

or just _____. The best bus to take is the
(present-tense verb)

one that leaves at _____:30 P.M. It's not very
(single-digit number greater than 1)

crowded or _____. It arrives half an hour later,
(adjective)

which is really _____. And a ticket only costs
(adjective)

_____.
(money amount)

What time does the
bus get to its destination? _____

Name: _____   Date: _____

My Older Sister

My older sister is very interesting.

She likes to _____
(present-tense verb)

and _____. She also
(present-tense verb)

is good at _____. But most of all, she loves to talk on the
(verb ending in -ing)

phone. The other night she got on at _____ o'clock P.M. and
(number from 1 to 12)

didn't get off until _____ and a half hours later. I think
(single-digit number greater than 1)

she was talking to _____. They talk all the time about
(name of a famous person)

_____ and _____. I think that kind
(plural noun)   (plural noun)

of stuff is so _____.
(adjective)

What time did the
sister get off the phone? _____

Name: _____ Date: _____

Babysitting

I was babysitting for the

_____ family last week.
(last name of a boy or girl)

They have _____
(single-digit number greater than 1)

children. We watched the _____ and played
(noun)

_____ and _____. I gave them
(name of a game)   (name of a game)

some _____ for a snack. Then I told them the story
(type of food)

of the three little _____. I started babysitting at
(type of animal, plural)

_____ :15 P.M. and worked for _____
(number from 1 to 12)   (single-digit number greater than 1)

hours. They paid me _____, which was really
(money amount)

_____.
(adjective)

What time did the
babysitter finish? _____

Name: _____   Date: _____

Singing Contest

_____
(first and last name of a girl)

is a very good singer. She sings

songs like "Row, Row, Row Your

_____." She also sings
(noun)

more _____ songs like "I Love _____."
(adjective)   (plural noun)

She was in a contest to see who could sing for the longest time. She

started at _____:30 A.M. and lasted for 15 minutes.
(single-digit number greater than 1)

Her voice was incredibly _____. One of the judges
(adjective)

_____ when he heard her. She won _____
(verb ending in -ed)   (ordinal number)

place and was awarded a trip to _____.
(name of a place)

What time did the
singer finish singing? _____

Name: _____   Date: _____

Haircut

I go to _____
(first name of a boy)

the Barber to get my hair cut. He really

does the most _____
(adjective)

job. This time, I asked him to make me look like _____.
(name of a famous person)

I got to the shop at _____:45 P.M. There were
(single-digit number greater than 1)

_____ people ahead of me. Each one took 15 minutes.
(single-digit number greater than 1)

That was okay. I just read magazines like _____ and
(type of animal)

Ranger _____. When my haircut was finished, I
(first name of a boy or girl)

really looked _____.
(adjective)

What time did the boy
finally get his hair cut? _____

Name: _____ Date: _____

Airplane Flight

Our family decided to fly to

_____. Each plane
(name of a place)

ticket cost _____ and
(money amount)

we needed _____
(single-digit number greater than 1)

tickets. Our flight left at _____ o'clock in the morning and lasted
(number from 1 to 12)

one hour and _____ minutes. During the flight, we watched
(double-digit number less than 50)

the movie *Return of the* _____. We also had snacks like
(plural noun)

_____ and _____. The pilot told me
(type of food)   (type of liquid)

I looked very _____. I guess that's because I was wearing
(adjective)

my _____ _____.
(color)   (type of clothing)

What time did
the flight end? _____

Name: _____   Date: _____

World Record

I thought it would be fun to

try to break the world record for

_____. So I asked
(verb ending in -ing)

my friend _____
(name of a boy or girl)

to time me. I started at _____ o'clock in the morning. I
(number from 1 to 12)

kept going for a record-breaking _____ minutes! I won two
(double-digit number)

_____ and a great _____. Wow!
(plural noun)   (noun)

Tomorrow I'm going to try to break the record for _____.
(different verb ending in -ing)

Since I already know how to _____, that should be easy!
(present-tense verb)

What time did the
record breaker finish? _____

Name: _____   Date: _____

Cleaning Up

My mom told my sister,

_____, and I that we
(name of a girl)

had to clean our rooms. Our rooms did

look pretty _____.
(adjective)

I had a pile of _____ on my floor. My sister had
(plural noun)

_____ everywhere. We started at 1 P.M. and worked
(plural noun)

together. I dusted all of the _____, and my sister
(type of furniture)

washed the _____. Then, of course, we had to
(plural noun)

_____ the _____, so we didn't finish
(present-tense verb)   (noun)

that day until _____ P.M. When we were finished, our mom said, "
(number from 2 to 11)

_____!"
(exclamation)

How long did it take the
kids to clean their rooms? _____

Name: _____   Date: _____

Train Ride

The _____
        (adjective)

Express leaves _____-ville Station every day
                (last name of a boy or girl)

at _____ o'clock in the morning. The train is
   (single-digit number)

ultra-modern, with _____ seats and personal
                    (adjective)

_____. It is powered by _____.
    (plural noun)   (plural noun)

It travels _____ miles per hour. It arrives at
            (number greater than 1)

_____ Town at _____ P.M.
  (last name of a boy or girl)   (single-digit number)

The ride is _____ and very _____.
             (adjective)   (adjective)

A round-trip ticket only costs _____ dollars!
                                (number greater than 1)

How many hours long
is the train ride? _____

Name: _____   Date: _____

Linear Measurement: Inches and Feet

Tale of the Dragon's Tail

There is an old _____
(adjective)

legend, from the Land of the _____, about a dragon
(plural noun)

known as _____ _____.
(adjective)   (first and last name of a boy)

This dragon lived in a cave. He terrorized the local village by eating all the

_____. He had a huge mouth with _____
(plural noun)   (number greater than 1)

teeth. His tail was _____ inches long. Fortunately, Brave
(double-digit number greater than 12)

Sir _____ fought the dragon and drove him out of the
(name of a boy)

land and far away to _____.
(name of a place)

Was the dragon's tail longer than a foot? _____

If so, how much longer? _____

Name: _____   Date: _____

Amazing Rescue

An amazing rescue took place yesterday

at _____ Canyon.
　　(last name of a boy or girl)

A cat named _____
　　　　　(name of a boy or girl)

was stuck at the bottom of the canyon.

Students from _____ happened to be there on a field trip.
　　　　　(name of a school)

Their teacher, Mr. _____, had _____
　　　　　(last name of a famous male)　　　　　(single-digit number greater than 1)

students remove their belts. Each belt was _____ inches
　　　　　　　　　　　　　　　　　(double-digit number less than 15)

long. The teacher linked them together to form a rescue rope. The cat grabbed

on and was brought up safely. The cat's owner, _____,
　　　　　　　　　　　　　　　　　　　(name of a famous person)

gave the class a really _____ _____
　　　　　　　　　　　(adjective)　　　　　　　　(noun)

as a reward.

Solve This!

How long was the rescue rope?
Answer in feet and inches. _____

Name: _____ Date: _____

Worms for Sale

My Uncle _____
(first name of a boy)

and I raise earthworms. People can buy our

worms for their gardens. Our worms make

_____ and _____ grow really big.
(type of plant, plural)   (type of plant, plural)

We line up the worms end-to-end and charge by the inch. Our first customer

only wanted worms that were _____ inches long. We
(single-digit number greater than 1)

found _____ worms that size for him. He said, "I'll take
(single-digit number greater than 1)

them! Your worms are the _____ I've seen!"
(adjective ending in -est)

How long were the worms altogether?
Answer in feet and inches. _____

Name: _____   Date: _____

Basketball Star

_____
(first and last name of a girl)

is quite a basketball star. She scored

_____ points in one
(number greater than 1)

game! She can dribble the ball

with her _____. She can even shoot with her left
(name of a body part)

_____. And she's so tall, she can touch the basket with her
(name of a body part)

_____. Two years ago, she was _____
(name of a body part)   (single-digit number from 2 to 5)

feet tall. She grew _____ inches the next year. This year she
(number from 2 to 13)

has grown another _____ inches. There aren't too many
(number from 2 to 13)

players as good as her, except for _____, of course.
(name of a famous person)

Solve This!

How tall is the basketball star?

Answer in feet and inches. _____

Name: _____   Date: _____

Snail Race

My friend _____
(name of a girl)

and I both have pet snails. My snail is

named _____. Her
(name of a famous person)

snail is called _____.
(name of a famous person)

One day we decided to race our snails. We lined them up side by side and said,

"Go!" Every five minutes, my snail went _____ inches.
(number from 2 to 9)

Every five minutes, her snail went _____ inches. The race
(different number from 2 to 9)

lasted _____ minutes. I guess you know who won.
(choose a number: 10, 15, or 20)

Which snail won the race? _____
How far did the winning snail go?
Answer in feet and inches. _____

Name: _____ Date: _____

Building a Boat

My class is building a boat. We have

named it the *S. S.* _____.
(noun)

We are using wood and _____. We plan to sail it on
(plural noun)

_____ Lake and possibly the _____
(last name of a boy or girl)(last name of a boy or girl)

River. We need a lot of wood. _____ brought in a board
(name of a girl)

that was _____ inches long. _____
(double-digit number less than 50)(name of a boy)

brought in a board that was _____
(double-digit number from 13 to 49)

inches long. That's all the wood we have so far, but we are going to buy

more. We are going to raise money by selling _____
(adjective)

_____ during lunch. I'm sure we'll make enough
(plural noun)

money in no time!

Solve This! What is the combined length of the wood the
boat builders have so far?
Answer in feet and inches. _____

Name: _____ Date: _____

Linear Measurement: Feet and Yards

Skateboard Shop

My name is

_____,
(first and last name of a boy or girl)

and I make _____
                    (adjective)

skateboards in my famous shop, the _____ Board.
                                            (adjective)

I only use wood from _____ trees and wheels made
                              (adjective)

of _____. I hand-paint my boards with all kinds
        (type of substance)

of cool graphics. My favorite designs have _____ and
                                                    (plural noun)

_____. Last week, I made _____ boards.
     (plural noun)   (number from 6 to 9)

Each board was _____ feet long. These boards were totally
                    (number from 1 to 4)

_____!
     (adjective)

What is the combined length
of wood the skateboard maker
used last week?
Answer in yards and feet. _____

50 Fill-In Math Word Problems: Time & Measurement: Grades 2–3 © 2009 by Bob Krech and Joan Novelli, Scholastic Teaching Resources

Name: _____   Date: _____

The Bridge

Our _____ Scout
(type of animal)

Troop has a new project. We have to build a

bridge across _____ Pond.
(last name of a boy or girl)

We began by using a long _____ to measure halfway across
(noun)

the pond. It was _____ feet long. Now we are ready to build.
(double-digit number less than 20)

We'll have to use _____, _____, and
(plural noun)   (plural noun)

_____. That's going to be so _____!
(plural noun)   (adjective)

It's a good thing we have plenty of _____. We figure it
(type of tool, plural)

will only take about _____ hours.
(number greater than 1)

How long should the bridge be?
Answer in yards and feet. _____

Name: _____   Date: _____

Olympic Throw

My cousin _____
                    (name of a boy)

is quite an athlete. He entered the

_____ Olympics. He ran
        (name of a town)

the _____-yard dash in _____ seconds.
        (double-digit number)   (single-digit number greater than 1)

He was also in the _____ Throw. That is a really
                            (noun)

_____ event. He had to do three throws. The total
        (adjective)

distance was his score. His first throw was _____ feet.
                                                (single-digit number greater than 1)

His second throw was _____ feet. His third throw was
                            (single-digit number greater than 1)

_____ feet. That score landed him in _____
    (single-digit number greater than 1)   (ordinal number)

place! In fact he was awarded a bronze _____!
                                                (noun)

What was the athlete's total
distance in the Throw?
Answer in yards and feet. _____

Name: _____   Date: _____

New Sneakers

I just joined the

_____ All-Stars
(name of a town)

basketball team. Our team is called the

_____. We got cool
(type of animal, plural)

uniforms with _____ _____ on the
(color)   (plural noun)

front and our names on the back. I am number _____. We also have
(any number)

special sneakers for games. They are the _____ model,
(name of a famous person)

with pictures of _____ _____ all over
(color)   (plural noun)

them. My sneakers are _____ centimeters long. When my
(double-digit number less than 50)

friends saw them, they all said, "_____!"
(exclamation)

Solve This! Are the new sneakers shorter than your feet? Explain. _____

_____

Name: _____   Date: _____

Linear Measurement: Centimeters and Meters

Special Pencil

I got a special pencil for my

_____ birthday.
(ordinal number)

The pencil is _____ and _____
            (color)   (color)

and has pictures of _____ all over it. The pencil
                     (plural noun)

by itself is _____ centimeters long. I added a fun
            (single-digit number greater than 1)

_____-shaped eraser. The eraser is
            (noun)

_____ centimeters long. Then I attached a miniature
(single-digit number greater than 1)

electronic _____ to the end of the eraser. That is
            (noun)

_____ centimeters long. Now my pencil is really special
(single-digit number greater than 1)

and _____, too!
      (adjective)

Solve This!

Is the entire special pencil
longer than your hand? Explain. _____

_____

50 Fill-In Math Word Problems: Time & Measurement: Grades 2–3 © 2009 by Bob Krech and Joan Novelli, Scholastic Teaching Resources

Name: _____   Date: _____

Linear Measurement: Centimeters and Meters

A Good Friend

My name is _____.
(short first name)

My good friends, _____
(name of a girl)

and _____, wanted to
(name of a boy)

surprise me on my birthday. Usually, they just give me chocolate

_____ or fresh-picked _____.
(type of dessert, plural)   (type of fruit, plural)

But this time, they spelled my name using sticks. Each stick was only

_____ centimeters long. Just to make the first letter in my
(single-digit number greater than 1)

name took _____ sticks! I'll bet they're glad
(double-digit number from 51 to 79)

my name isn't _____!
(long first name)

What was the combined length of the sticks
used to make the first letter? Answer in meters and
centimeters.

_____

Name: _____ Date: _____

Class Banner

I 'm in Ms. _____'s
(last name of a girl)

_____-grade class. We wanted
(ordinal number)

to make a class banner to celebrate

_____ Day. We used
(noun)

crayons, markers, _____, and _____.
(plural noun)   (plural noun)

The banner was divided into 10 sections, one for each student to decorate.

Each section was _____ centimeters long. I drew a fancy
(double-digit number less than 20)

_____ on my section and made _____
(noun)   (adjective)

_____ all around it. I also wrote the words
(plural noun)

"_____" under the picture.
(old saying)

This banner is going to be very _____!
(adjective)

Solve This!

How long was the banner?
Answer in meters and centimeters. _____

50 Fill-In Math Word Problems: Time & Measurement: Grades 2–3 © 2009 by Bob Krech and Joan Novelli, Scholastic Teaching Resources

Name: _____   Date: _____

Linear Measurement: Centimeters and Meters

Ponytail

T he famous _____,
(type of job)

_____,
(first and last name of a girl)

decided she needed a new look. She started

by wearing _____
(color)

jeans and _____ sneakers. Then she decided to
(color)

grow a ponytail. It took her _____ months. It grew
(single-digit number greater than 1)

_____ centimeters each month. She likes to put
(number from 4 to 9)

_____ _____ in it. She was recently
(adjective)   (plural noun)

featured in _____ for this exciting new style.
(name of a magazine)

Is the ponytail shorter than a meter? _____

If so, how much shorter? _____

Name: _____   Date: _____

Doghouse

I built my dog, _____,
(name of a famous person)

a doghouse. It is two stories high! I painted

the whole thing _____
(color)

and _____. The first story is _____
(color)   (double-digit number)

centimeters high. My dog keeps his _____ and
(plural noun)

_____ in there. The second story is _____
(plural noun)   (double-digit number)

centimeters high. That's where my dog likes to _____
(present-tense verb)

and _____. I can tell my dog really loves this house.
(present-tense verb)

He always starts _____ when he gets close!
(verb ending in -ing)

Is the doghouse higher than a meter? _____

If so, how much higher? _____

Name: _____   Date: _____

Party Game

I learned a new game at my friend

_____'s
(name of a girl)

birthday party. It's called Roll It. You

need one _____
                    (adjective)

_____ that weighs about _____ pounds. You
        (noun)   (number greater than 1)

roll it as far as you can. You do that _____ times and then
                                        (single-digit number greater than 1)

add up the distances of your rolls. I rolled it _____
                                                    (number from 10 and 20)

centimeters each time. I won a prize bag full of my favorite

_____! We also played Musical _____
        (plural noun)   (plural noun)

and Pin the Tail on the _____. But I loved Roll It the best!
                              (noun)

Solve This!   What was the combined
total of the rolled distances?
Answer in meters and centimeters. _____

Name: _____   Date: _____

Super Sub

We had an end-of-the-year party for

our class. To help, we all brought in food.

I brought fried _____.
                                    (type of food)

My friend _____ brought baked
                    (name of a boy or girl)

_____. There was plenty of _____
            (type of food)   (type of liquid)

to drink. We played music, like the new hit song, "Moon Over

_____." Our teacher brought in a giant sub sandwich
            (name of a town)

for us all to share. Each of us got a piece that was _____
                                                                            (number from 6 to 9)

centimeters long, and there are _____ of us. That's a
                                            (double-digit number less than 20)

lot of sandwich!

How long was the sandwich?
Answer in meters
and centimeters. _____

Name: _____ Date: _____

Dream House

I'm saving up to build a dream house for

my dolls. So far I have _____

(number greater than 1)

dollars. The house will be _____

(number greater than 1)

feet high and have _____

(number greater than 1)

windows. It will have automatic _____ and electric

(plural noun)

_____. I am working on the plans with my architect,

(plural noun)

_____. She says the base of the house

(first and last name of a girl)

should have a length of _____ feet and a width

(single-digit number greater than 1)

of _____ feet. This is going to be the most

(single-digit number greater than 1)

_____ house ever built!

(adjective)

What will be the area of
the base of the house? _____

50 Fill-In Math Word Problems: Time & Measurement: Grades 2–3 © 2009 by Bob Krech and Joan Novelli, Scholastic Teaching Resources

Name: _____   Date: _____

Swimming Pool

A new town pool just opened in

_____.
(name of a town)

It's in the shape of a rectangle and is

_____ feet wide
(double-digit number less than 30)

and _____ feet long. There is a diving board
(double-digit number between 30 and 40)

and also a funny _____-shaped fountain that sprays
(noun)

water for the little kids. The _____ snack bar serves
(adjective)

delicious _____ and _____
(type of food)   (type of food)

and the best _____. _____ is a
(type of food)   (name of a boy or girl)

lifeguard there, and so is _____. I love to go there and
(name of a boy or girl)

_____ all day.
(present-tense verb)

What is the perimeter of the pool? _____

Name: _____   Date: _____

Big Burger

_____'s Restaurant
(name of a boy)

is selling a new sandwich. It's called

the Big _____
(adjective)

Burger. The burger patty is made

with _____ ounces of beef. The chef also mixes in
(number from 6 to 9)

_____ ounces of _____ and
(number from 6 to 9)   (type of food)

_____ ounces of _____ .
(number from 6 to 9)   (type of food)

The burger is grilled for _____ minutes. It's served on a big
(number greater than 1)

_____ with _____ on top. It tastes so
(noun)   (type of vegetable, plural)

_____ , it makes me want to _____ .
(adjective)   (present-tense verb)

How much does the
burger patty weigh?
Answer in pounds
and ounces. _____

Name: _____ **Date:** _____

Lots of Laundry

My mom said that my brother,

_____, my sister,
(name of a boy)

_____, and I
(name of a girl)

all have to do our own laundry now.

My laundry weighed _____ pounds. My brother's
(number from 6 to 9)

weighed _____ pounds. Meanwhile, my sister's weighed
(number from 6 to 9)

_____ ounces. We put our laundry in the
(number from 16 to 29)

_____ and poured in _____ ounces
(type of appliance)   (single-digit number greater than 1)

of detergent. I must say our clothes came out really _____
(adjective)

and _____.
(adjective)

Solve This! How much did the laundry
weigh altogether?
Answer in pounds and ounces. _____

Name: _____   Date: _____

Peanut Lover

My dad loves peanuts. He also

loves _____,
　　　　　　(type of food)

but peanuts are his favorite snack.

When he watches *The Adventures of*

_____ on TV, he always has a _____
(name of a famous person)　　　　　　　　　　　　　　(type of container)

of peanuts. Last week, he ate _____ ounces each
　　　　　　　　　　　　　(double-digit number less than 20)

night for _____ nights. He also always drinks
　　　　　(number from 2 to 6)

_____ Cola with his snack. It's actually healthy
(last name of a boy or girl)

because it's made from _____. He says it tastes
　　　　　　　　　　　　(type of fruit, plural)

_____!
　　(adjective)

How many pounds and ounces
of peanuts did the dad eat? _____

Weight Measurement: Ounces and Pounds

Hiking

Last week I went on a long hike to

_____.
(name of a town)

It took _____ hours.
(single-digit number greater than 1)

The weather was _____
(adjective)

and _____. The temperature was _____
(adjective)   (double-digit number)

degrees! My pack was really heavy because I brought my

_____ and some _____. It weighed
(plural noun)   (plural noun)

_____ pounds. I did get to see _____
(number from 2 to 10)   (last name of a boy or girl)

Falls and _____ Creek. By then, I was so hot I
(last name of a famous person)

_____ into the water.
(past-tense verb)

Solve This!   How many ounces
did the pack weigh? _____

Name: _____   Date: _____

Weight Measurement: Grams and Kilograms

Cherry Picking

W e went cherry picking at

_____'s Farm.
(name of a famous person)

This farm also sells _____
(plural noun)

and _____. Each cherry we picked weighed
(plural noun)

_____ grams. I picked
(number from 4 to 8)

_____ cherries. My friend _____
(single-digit number greater than 1)   (name of a girl)

picked _____ cherries. My other friend,
(single-digit number greater than 1)

_____, picked _____ cherries.
(name of a boy)   (single-digit number greater than 1)

When we got home, we decided to use them to make

_____. Delicious!
(type of food)

What was the total weight in grams
of all the cherries picked? _____

Name: _____ Date: _____

Weightlifting

_____ is a professional
(name of a boy)

weightlifter from _____.
(name of a country)

He finished _____ in his
(ordinal number)

last competition. To stay strong, he

eats a dozen _____ for breakfast every day and drinks
(plural noun)

_____ gallons of _____. Yesterday
(single-digit number greater than 1)   (type of liquid)

he lifted a single _____ that weighed _____
(noun)   (number from 1 to 51)

kilograms. That was with his left hand! Then he put another one of the

same weight in his right hand and lifted them both together! He is really

_____.
(adjective)

Solve This!

How much did he lift with his
left and right hand together?

Answer in grams. _____

Would that be hard to do? Explain. _____

_____

Name: _____   Date: _____

Weight Measurement: Grams and Kilograms

Grocery Shopping

Last night, my mom and I went

shopping at my favorite grocery store,

_____'s Supermarket.
　　(last name of a boy or girl)

We bought _____ kilograms of
　　　　　(single-digit number greater than 1)

_____ and _____ kilograms of
　(type of food)　　　　　　　　(single-digit number greater than 1)

_____. Then we got _____
　(type of food)　　　　　　　　　　　　　(number from 20 to 80)

grams of _____. It only cost _____,
　　　　　(type of food)　　　　　　　　　　　(money amount)

and we got a free _____ for shopping there. It is the most
　　　　　　　　　　(noun)

_____ store!
　(adjective)

How much did the groceries
weigh altogether? Answer in
kilograms and grams. _____

Name: _____   Date: _____

Movie Treats

I was going to see the new movie,

_____'s
(name of a boy)

_____ *Adventure*.
(adjective)

It is supposed to be really, super _____. I stocked
(adjective)

up on some candy first. I bought _____ grams
(triple-digit number greater than 500)

of Chewy _____ Drops. I also got
(type of fruit)

_____ grams of _____ Squares.
(triple-digit number greater than 500)   (type of food)

The candy was so _____, I ate it in
(adjective)

_____ minutes.
(number greater than 1)

How much did the candy
weigh altogether? Answer in
kilograms and grams. _____

Name: _____ Date: _____

Lemonade Stand

My friend _____
(name of a girl)

and I have a lemonade stand. We sell lemonade

and _____.
(type of food)

Our sales slogan is "Our lemonade tastes better than

_____!" Today we took orders for _____
(plural noun)   (double-digit number less than 20)

eight-ounce cups of lemonade. _____ of those were
(single-digit number greater than 1)

ordered by _____. He loves it and says it tastes really
(name of a boy)

_____. We've made _____ already!
(adjective)   (money amount)

How many fluid ounces of
lemonade did the friends serve? _____

Name: _____ Date: _____

Milk for Lunch

_____ and
(name of a boy)

his _____
(type of sport)

team sit together at lunchtime. They eat

mostly _____
(type of food)

sandwiches and _____ chips. They like to drink
(type of vegetable)

_____ milk. Today there were _____
(flavor)   (single-digit number greater than 1)

team members at the lunch table, and they each drank _____
(number from 2 to 5)

cups of milk. They say it makes them _____.
(adjective)

How many pints of milk did
the team members drink altogether? _____

Name: _____   Date: _____

Car Trip

We went on a car trip to

_____.
(name of a town)

That is about _____
(triple-digit number)

miles away so we really had to

prepare. There are _____ of us kids. Our parents
(single-digit number greater than 2)

packed up _____ and _____
(type of food)   (name of a game)

for the ride. They also got each of us _____ cups of
(single-digit number greater than 1)

_____ juice. We saw some cool stuff along the way.
(type of fruit)

There was the _____ River and the
(name of a place)

_____ Bridge. When we finally got there, we all
(last name of a famous person)

shouted, " _____!"
(exclamation)

Solve This!   How much juice did they
have altogether? Answer in
pints and cups. _____

Name: _____   Date: _____

Secret Sauce

Chef _____
(first name of a boy)

has a TV show called *Cooking and*

_____ *With the Chef.*
(verb ending in *-ing*)

He loves to cook _____ and Baked
(type of food)

_____. Right now he is grilling a lot. He grills
(type of food)

_____ and _____. He always puts his
(type of food, plural)   (type of food, plural)

special Secret Sauce on everything when he grills. Today he put it all over

_____ and grilled them for _____ hours.
(type of food, plural)   (number greater than 1)

Wow! They looked _____! He uses so much, he needs
(adjective)

_____ quarts of the sauce for every show.
(number from 6 to 9)

How much secret sauce does
the chef make for each show?
Answer in gallons and quarts. _____

Name: _____   Date: _____

Liquid Measurement: Quarts and Half Gallons

Football Game

We had a football game Saturday

against the _____
                        (name of a town)

_____. It was very hot,
     (type of animal, plural)

probably _____ degrees!
              (number greater than 80)

Fortunately, we had plenty of _____-ade to drink. I like
                                        (type of animal)

the _____ flavor best. We have_____
              (flavor)   (number from 6 to 9)

players on our team, and each of us got a quart-size bottle. At halftime,

the score was _____ points to _____. We scored
                (number greater than 1)   (number greater than 1)

_____ in the second half, and they never scored again. It was a
 (number greater than 1)

close game!

Solve This!

How much was there to
drink altogether? Answer in
half gallons and quarts. _____

Name: _____   Date: _____

Soup for Dinner

My two sisters and I love to make

soup for dinner. We call our soup

_____ Surprise Soup.
(name of a place)

We put in _____, _____,
(type of liquid)   (type of vegetable, plural)

_____, and _____. We cook it for
(type of food)   (plural noun)

_____ hours on the _____. You have to stir it at
(number greater than 1)   (noun)

least _____ times for it to be nice and _____.
(number greater than 1)   (adjective)

When the soup is finished, there are _____ liters for
(choose a number: 2, 3, or 4)

each of us.

How many milliliters of
soup do the sisters make? _____

Liquid Measurement: Milliliters and Liters

Gluey Projects

Our class is doing a really

_____ project in art.
(adjective)

Our teacher gave us _____,
(type of substance)

_____, and _____. We put it
(common household material)   (plural noun)

all together to make model _____. It takes lots of
(plural noun)

glue to hold everything together. In fact, the kids at each table used

one _____-milliliter bottle of glue. There are
(choose a number: 200, 300, 400, or 500)

_____ tables. So that's a lot of glue!
(number from 5 to 9)

How much glue did the class use?

Answer in liters and milliliters. _____

Name: _____ Date: _____

Secret Ingredient

My Grandma _____
(first name of a girl)

makes the best iced tea. She says the

recipe was handed down to her from her

Great-Grandma _____. First, she says, the tea has
(first name of a girl)

to come from _____. You add a lot of ice to the
(name of a place)

tea and _____ lemons. Of course, you need sugar, too. The
(number greater than 1)

recipe makes _____ milliliters, and Grandma puts in
(quadruple-digit number)

_____ teaspoons of sugar for all of that. There's one
(single-digit number greater than 1)

more ingredient, but Grandma says it's a secret. I'm not sure, but I think

it's _____. That must be what makes the iced tea so
(type of food)

_____.
(adjective)

How many liter containers would
they need to hold all the iced tea? _____

 50 Fill-In Math Word Problems: Time & Measurement: Grades 2–3 © 2009 by Bob Krech and Joan Novelli, Scholastic Teaching Resources